Bescherelle 2024

(English Edition)

Learn French Easily

Chapter 1: Introduction to the 1st Group Verbs 2

    1.1 Definition and Characteristics 3

    1.2 Conjugation Patterns 3

    1.3 Past Tense (Passé Composé)...................................4

    1.4 Future Tense 5

    1.5 Exercises 5

Chapter 2: Introduction to the 2nd Group Verbs 6

    2.1 Definition and Characteristics 6

    2.2 Conjugation Patterns 7

    2.3 Past Tense (Passé Composé)...................................8

    2.4 Future Tense 8

    2.5 Exercises 9

Chapter 3: Introduction to the 3rd Group Verbs...............................9

    3.1 Definition and Characteristics 9

    3.2 Conjugation Patterns...10

    3.3 Past Tense (Passé Composé)...................................12

    3.4 Future Tense 12

    3.5 Exercises 13

Chapter 4: Irregular Verbs 13

    4.1 Definition and Characteristics 13

    4.2 Conjugation Patterns...14

    4.3 Past Tense (Passé Composé)...................................16

    4.4 Future Tense 17

    4.5 Exercises 17

Chapter 5: Indicative Tenses..18

5.1 Present Tense 18

5.2 Past Tense (Passé Composé)..19

5.3 Future Tense 21

The future tense is used to describe actions that will happen in the future. Here are some examples for each group of verbs: 21

5.4 Imperfect Tense..22

5.5 Pluperfect Tense...24

5.6 Future Perfect Tense..25

5.7 Exercises 26

Chapter 6: The Subjunctive 27

6.1 Definition and Characteristics 27

6.2 Conjugation Patterns...27

6.3 Uses of the Subjunctive...30

6.4 Exercises 30

Chapter 7: Compound Tenses...30

7.1 Definition and Characteristics 30

Chapter 7: Compound Tenses...31

7.2 Present Perfect (Passé Composé) 31

7.3 Pluperfect (Plus-que-parfait) 33

7.4 Future Perfect (Futur Antérieur) 35

7.5 Conditional Perfect (Conditionnel Passé) 37

7.6 Exercises 39

Chapter 8: Non-Personal Forms...39

8.1 Infinitive 40

8.2 Present Participle...40

8.3 Past Participle..41

8.4 Gerund 41

8.5 Exercises 42

Chapter 9: Special Conjugations 42

9.1 Reflexive Verbs 42

9.2 Impersonal Verbs...43

9.3 Defective Verbs..44

9.4 Exercises 45

Chapter 10: Exercises and Practice....................................45

10.1 Introduction to Exercises..45

10.2 Exercises on 1st Group Verbs..45

10.3 Exercises on 2nd Group Verbs.......................................47

10.4 Exercises on 3rd Group Verbs 50

10.5 Exercises on Irregular Verbs 52

10.6 Exercises on Compound Tenses......................................54

10.7 Conclusion of the Chapter 55

Chapter 11: Appendices 55

11.1 List of Irregular Verbs...56

11.2 Summary Tables 57

Chapter 12: Verbs with Particles...60

12.1 Definition and Characteristics 60

12.2 Conjugation Patterns...61

12.3 Exercises 62

Chapter 13: Conclusion 63

13.1 Summary of Key Points 63

13.2 Encouragement for Continued Practice 63

Chapter 1: Introduction to the 1st Group Verbs

1.1 Definition and Characteristics

The 1st group verbs are regular verbs that end in -er in their infinitive form. They follow a predictable conjugation pattern, making them easier to learn. Here are some examples:

Verb	Infinitive	Present (I)	Past (I)	Future (I)
To love	aimer	j'ai me	j'ai ai mé	j'ai mer ai
To play	jouer	je joue	j'ai jo ué	je jou erai
To dance	danser	je danse	j'ai da ns é	je dan ser ai

1.2 Conjugation Patterns

The present tense conjugation for 1st group verbs is as follows:

Pronoun	Ending
I	-e
You (singular)	-es
He/She/It	-e
We	-ons
You (plural)	-ez
They	-ent

Examples:

- I love: j'aime
- You play: tu joues
- He dances: il danse

1.3 Past Tense (Passé Composé)

The past tense (passé composé) for 1st group verbs is formed with the auxiliary verb "avoir" and the past participle. Here are some examples:

Verb	Infinitive	Past Participle	Past (I)
To love	aimer	aimé	j'ai aimé
To play	jouer	joué	j'ai joué
To dance	danser	dansé	j'ai dansé

Examples:

- I loved: j'ai aimé
- You played: tu as joué
- He danced: il a dansé

1.4 Future Tense

The future tense for 1st group verbs is formed by adding the future endings to the infinitive form of the verb. Here are some examples:

Verb	Infinitive	Future (I)
To love	aimer	j'aimerai
To play	jouer	je jouerai
To dance	danser	je danserai

Examples:

- I will love: j'aimerai
- You will play: tu joueras
- He will dance: il dansera

1.5 Exercises

To reinforce your understanding, here are some exercises:

1. Conjugate the verb "aimer" in the present tense.
2. Conjugate the verb "jouer" in the past tense.
3. Conjugate the verb "danser" in the future tense.

Chapter 2: Introduction to the 2nd Group Verbs

2.1 Definition and Characteristics

The 2nd group verbs are regular verbs that end in -ir in their infinitive form and have their present participle ending in -issant. They follow a predictable conjugation pattern. Here are some examples:

Verb	Infinitive	Present (I)	Past (I)	Future (I)
To finish	finir	je finis	j'ai fini	je finirai
To choose	choisir	je choisis	j'ai choisi	je choisirai
To succeed	réussir	je réussis	j'ai réussi	je réussirai

si

2.2 Conjugation Patterns

The present tense conjugation for 2nd group verbs is as follows:

Pronoun	Ending
I	-is
You (singular)	-is
He/She/It	-it
We	-issons
You (plural)	-issez
They	-isse

		nt	

Examples:

- I finish: je finis
- You choose: tu choisis
- He succeeds: il réussit

2.3 Past Tense (Passé Composé)

The past tense (passé composé) for 2nd group verbs is formed with the auxiliary verb "avoir" and the past participle. Here are some examples:

Verb	Infinitive	Past Participle	Past (I)
To finish	finir	fini	j'ai fini
To choose	choisir	choisi	j'ai choisi
To succeed	réussir	réussi	j'ai réussi

Examples:

- I finished: j'ai fini
- You chose: tu as choisi
- He succeeded: il a réussi

2.4 Future Tense

The future tense for 2nd group verbs is formed by adding the future endings to the infinitive form of the verb. Here are some examples:

Verb	Infinitive	Future (I)
To finish	finir	je finirai
To choose	choisir	je choisirai
To succeed	réussir	je réussirai

Examples:

- I will finish: je finirai
- You will choose: tu choisiras
- He will succeed: il réussira

2.5 Exercises

To reinforce your understanding, here are some exercises:

4. Conjugate the verb "finir" in the present tense.
5. Conjugate the verb "choisir" in the past tense.
6. Conjugate the verb "réussir" in the future tense.

Chapter 3: Introduction to the 3rd Group Verbs

3.1 Definition and Characteristics

The 3rd group verbs are irregular verbs that do not follow the patterns of the 1st and 2nd groups. They include verbs ending in -ir, -oir, -re, and some -er verbs. Here are some examples:

Verb	Infinitive	Present (I)	Past (I)	Future (I)
To go	aller	je vais	je suis allé(e)	j'irai
To take	prendre	je prends	j'ai pris	je prendrai
To see	voir	je vois	j'ai vu	je verrai

3.2 Conjugation Patterns

The present tense conjugation for 3rd group verbs varies. Here are some examples:

Aller (to go):

Pronoun	Conjugation
I	vais
You (singular)	vas
He/She/It	va
We	allons
You (plural)	allez
They	vont

Prendre (to take):

Pronoun	Conjugation
I	prends

You (singular)	prends
He/She/It	prend
We	prenons
You (plural)	prenez
They	prennent

Voir (to see):

Pronoun	Conjugation
I	vois
You (singular)	vois
He/She/It	voit
We	voyons

You (plural)	voyez
They	voient

3.3 Past Tense (Passé Composé)

The past tense (passé composé) for 3rd group verbs is formed with the auxiliary verb "avoir" or "être" and the past participle. Here are some examples:

Verb	Infinitive	Past Participle	Past (I)
To go	aller	allé	je suis allé(e)
To take	prendre	pris	j'ai pris
To see	voir	vu	j'ai vu

Examples:

- I went: je suis allé(e)
- You took: tu as pris
- He saw: il a vu

3.4 Future Tense

The future tense for 3rd group verbs is formed by adding the future endings to the infinitive form of the verb. Here are some examples:

Verb	Infinitive	Future (I)
To go	aller	j'irai
To take	prendre	je prendrai
To see	voir	je verrai

Examples:

- I will go: j'irai
- You will take: tu prendras
- He will see: il verra

3.5 Exercises

To reinforce your understanding, here are some exercises:

7. Conjugate the verb "aller" in the present tense.
8. Conjugate the verb "prendre" in the past tense.
9. Conjugate the verb "voir" in the future tense.

Chapter 4: Irregular Verbs

4.1 Definition and Characteristics

Irregular verbs do not follow the regular conjugation patterns of the 1st, 2nd, or 3rd groups. They have unique conjugations that must be memorized. Here are some examples:

Verb	Infinitive	Present (I)	Past (I)	Future (I)
To be	être	je suis	j'ai été	je serai
To have	avoir	j'ai	j'ai eu	j'aurai
To do	faire	je fais	j'ai fait	je ferai

4.2 Conjugation Patterns

The present tense conjugation for irregular verbs varies. Here are some examples:

Être (to be):

Pronoun	Conjugation
I	suis
You (singular)	es
He/She/It	est
We	sommes
You (plural)	êtes
They	sont

Avoir (to have):

Pronoun	Conjugation
I	ai

You (singular)	as
He/She /It	a
We	avons
You (plural)	avez
They	ont

Faire (to do):

Pronoun	Conjugation
I	fais
You (singular)	fais
He/She /It	fait
We	faisons
You	faites

(plural)	
They	font

4.3 Past Tense (Passé Composé)

The past tense (passé composé) for irregular verbs is formed with the auxiliary verb "avoir" and the past participle. Here are some examples:

Verb	Infinitive	Past Participle	Past (I)
To be	être	été	j'ai été
To have	avoir	eu	j'ai eu
To do	faire	fait	j'ai fait

Examples:

- I was: j'ai été
- You had: tu as eu
- He did: il a fait

4.4 Future Tense

The future tense for irregular verbs is formed by adding the future endings to the irregular stem of the verb. Here are some examples:

Verb	Infinitive	Future (I)
To be	être	je serai
To have	avoir	j'aurai
To do	faire	je ferai

Examples:

- I will be: je serai
- You will have: tu auras
- He will do: il fera

4.5 Exercises

To reinforce your understanding, here are some exercises:

10. Conjugate the verb "être" in the present tense.
11. Conjugate the verb "avoir" in the past tense.
12. Conjugate the verb "faire" in the future tense.

Chapter 5: Indicative Tenses

5.1 Present Tense

The present tense is used to describe actions that are currently happening or habitual actions. Here are some examples for each group of verbs:

1st Group Verbs:

Verb	Infinitive	Present (I)
To love	aimer	j'aime
To play	jouer	je joue
To dance	danser	je danse

2nd Group Verbs:

Verb	Infinitive	Present (I)
To finish	finir	je finis

To choose	choisir	je choisis
To succeed	réussir	je réussis

3rd Group Verbs:

Verb	Infinitive	Present (I)
To go	aller	je vais
To take	prendre	je prends
To see	voir	je vois

5.2 Past Tense (Passé Composé)

The past tense (passé composé) is used to describe actions that have been completed in the past. Here are some examples for each group of verbs:

1st Group Verbs:

Verb	Infinitive	Past Participle	Past (I)
To love	aimer	aimé	j'ai aimé
To play	jouer	joué	j'ai joué
To dance	danser	dansé	j'ai dansé

2nd Group Verbs:

Verb	Infinitive	Past Participle	Past (I)
To finish	finir	fini	j'ai fini
To	choisi	choisi	j'ai

choose	r		chois i
To succeed	réuss ir	réussi	j'ai réuss i

3rd Group Verbs:

Verb	Infinitive	Past Participle	Past (I)
To go	aller	allé	je suis allé(e)
To take	prendre	pris	j'ai pris
To see	voir	vu	j'ai vu

5.3 Future Tense

The future tense is used to describe actions that will happen in the future. Here are some examples for each group of verbs:

1st Group Verbs:

Verb	Infinitive	Future (I)
To love	aimer	j'aimerai
To play	jouer	je jouerai
To dance	danser	je danserai

2nd Group Verbs:

Verb	Infinitive	Future (I)
To finish	finir	je finirai
To choose	choisir	je choisirai

Verb	Infinitive	Future (I)
To succeed	réussir	je réussirai

3rd Group Verbs:

Verb	Infinitive	Future (I)
To go	aller	j'irai
To take	prendre	je prendrai
To see	voir	je verrai

5.4 Imperfect Tense

The imperfect tense is used to describe ongoing or habitual actions in the past. Here are some examples for each group of verbs:

1st Group Verbs:

Verb	Infinitive	Imperfect (I)
To love	aimer	j'aimais

To play	jouer	je jouais
To dance	danser	je dansais

2nd Group Verbs:

Verb	Infinitive	Imperfect (I)
To finish	finir	je finissais
To choose	choisir	je choisissais
To succeed	réussir	je réussissais

3rd Group Verbs:

Verb	Infinitive	Imperfect (I)
To go	aller	j'allais

Verb	Infinitive	Pluperfect (I)
To take	prendre	je prenais
To see	voir	je voyais

5.5 Pluperfect Tense

The pluperfect tense is used to describe actions that had been completed before another action in the past. Here are some examples for each group of verbs:

1st Group Verbs:

Verb	Infinitive	Pluperfect (I)
To love	aimer	j'avais aimé
To play	jouer	j'avais joué
To dance	danser	j'avais dansé

2nd Group Verbs:

Verb	Infinitive	Pluperfect (I)

Verb	Infinitive	Pluperfect (I)
To finish	finir	j'avais fini
To choose	choisir	j'avais choisi
To succeed	réussir	j'avais réussi

3rd Group Verbs:

Verb	Infinitive	Pluperfect (I)
To go	aller	j'étais allé(e)
To take	prendre	j'avais pris
To see	voir	j'avais vu

5.6 Future Perfect Tense

The future perfect tense is used to describe actions that will have been completed before a specific point in the future. Here are some examples for each group of verbs:

1st Group Verbs:

Verb	Infinitive	Future Perfect (I)
To love	aimer	j'aurai aimé
To play	jouer	j'aurai joué
To dance	danser	j'aurai dansé

2nd Group Verbs:

Verb	Infinitive	Future Perfect (I)
To finish	finir	j'aurai fini
To choose	choisir	j'aurai choisi
To succeed	réussir	j'aurai réussi

3rd Group Verbs:

Verb	Infinitive	Future Perfect (I)
To go	aller	je serai allé(e)
To take	prendre	j'aurai pris
To see	voir	j'aurai vu

5.7 Exercises

To reinforce your understanding, here are some exercises:

13. Conjugate the verb "aimer" in the imperfect tense.
14. Conjugate the verb "finir" in the pluperfect tense.
15. Conjugate the verb "aller" in the future perfect tense.

Chapter 6: The Subjunctive

6.1 Definition and Characteristics

The subjunctive mood is used to express doubt, emotion, necessity, or uncertainty. It is often found in dependent clauses introduced by "que" (that). Here are some examples:

Verb	Infinitive	Subjunctive (I)

To love	aimer	que j'aime
To finish	finir	que je finisse
To go	aller	que j'aille

6.2 Conjugation Patterns

The present subjunctive conjugation for each group of verbs is as follows:

1st Group Verbs:

Pronoun	Ending
I	-e
You (singular)	-es
He/She/It	-e
We	-

	ions
You (plural)	-iez
They	-ent

Examples:

- That I love: que j'aime
- That you play: que tu joues
- That he dances: qu'il danse

2nd Group Verbs:

Pronoun	Ending
I	-isse
You (singular)	-isses
He/She/It	-isse
We	-issions

Pronoun	Ending
You (plural)	-issiez
They	-issent

Examples:

- That I finish: que je finisse
- That you choose: que tu choisisses
- That he succeeds: qu'il réussisse

3rd Group Verbs:

Pronoun	Ending
I	-e
You (singular)	-es
He/She/It	-e
We	-ions

You (plural)	-iez
They	-ent

Examples:

- That I go: que j'aille
- That you take: que tu prennes
- That he sees: qu'il voie

6.3 Uses of the Subjunctive

The subjunctive is used in various contexts, such as expressing wishes, doubts, emotions, and necessities. Here are some examples:

- **Wishes**: Je souhaite que tu **réussisses**. (I wish that you succeed.)
- **Doubts**: Je doute qu'il **vienne**. (I doubt that he comes.)
- **Emotions**: Je suis heureux que tu **sois** ici. (I am happy that you are here.)
- **Necessities**: Il faut que nous **partions**. (We must leave.)

6.4 Exercises

To reinforce your understanding, here are some exercises:

16. Conjugate the verb "aimer" in the present subjunctive.
17. Conjugate the verb "finir" in the present subjunctive.
18. Conjugate the verb "aller" in the present subjunctive.

Chapter 7: Compound Tenses

7.1 Definition and Characteristics

Compound tenses are formed with an auxiliary verb (être or avoir) and the past participle of the main verb. They are used to express actions that are completed or have a specific relationship to another time. Here are some examples:

| Verb | Infinitive | Present Perfect (I) | Pl
uperfect (I) | Future Perfect (I) |
|---|---|---|---|---|
| To love | aimer | j'ai aimé | j'avais aimé | j'aurai aimé |
| To fi | finir | j'ai fini | j'avais fini | j'aurai fini |

n i s h				
T o g o	al le r	je suis allé(e)	j'éta is allé(e)	je serai allé(e)

Chapter 7: Compound Tenses

7.2 Present Perfect (Passé Composé)

The present perfect tense is used to describe actions that have been completed in the past. Here are some examples for each group of verbs:

2nd Group Verbs:

Verb	Infinitive	Past Participle	Present Perfect (I)
To finish	finir	fini	j'ai fini
To	ch	choisi	j'ai choisi

cho ose	ois ir		
To succ eed	réu ssir	réussi	j'ai réussi

3rd Group Verbs:

Verb	Infinitive	Past Participle	Present Perfect (I)
To go	aller	allé	je suis allé(e)
To take	prendre	pris	j'ai pris

Verb	Infinitive	Past Participle	Pluperfect (I)
k e			
T o s e e	voi r	vu	j'ai vu

7.3 Pluperfect (Plus-que-parfait)

The pluperfect tense is used to describe actions that had been completed before another action in the past. Here are some examples for each group of verbs:

1st Group Verbs:

Verb	Infinitive	Past Participle	Pluperfect (I)
To love	aimer	aimé	j'avais aimé
To play	jouer	joué	j'avais joué

Verb	Infinitive	Past Participle	Pluperfect (I)
To dance	danser	dansé	j'avais dansé

2nd Group Verbs:

Verb	Infinitive	Past Participle	Pluperfect (I)
To finish	finir	fini	j'avais fini
To choose	choisir	choisi	j'avais choisi
To succeed	réussir	réussi	j'avais réussi

3rd Group Verbs:

Verb	Infinitive	Past Participle	Pluperfect (I)

b	e		
T o g o	all er	allé	j'étais allé(e)
T o t a k e	pre ndr e	pris	j'avais pris
T o s e e	voi r	vu	j'avais vu

7.4 Future Perfect (Futur Antérieur)

The future perfect tense is used to describe actions that will have been completed before a specific point in the future. Here are some examples for each group of verbs:

1st Group Verbs:

Ve	Inf	Past	Future

rb	ini tiv e	Partici ple	Perfect (I)
To lo ve	ai me r	aimé	j'aurai aimé
To pl ay	jou er	joué	j'aurai joué
To da nc e	da nse r	dansé	j'aurai dansé

2nd Group Verbs:

Ver b	Inf ini tiv e	Past Partici ple	Future Perfect (I)
To finis h	fini r	fini	j'aurai fini
To cho	ch ois	choisi	j'aurai choisi

ose	ir		
To succ eed	réu ssir	réussi	j'aurai réussi

3rd Group Verbs:

V e r b	Inf ini tiv e	Past Partici ple	Future Perfect (I)
T o g o	all er	allé	je serai allé(e)
T o t a k e	pre ndr e	pris	j'aurai pris
T o s e e	voi r	vu	j'aurai vu

7.5 Conditional Perfect (Conditionnel Passé)

The conditional perfect tense is used to describe actions that would have been completed under certain conditions. Here are some examples for each group of verbs:

1st Group Verbs:

Verb	Infinitive	Past Participle	Conditional Perfect (I)
To love	aimer	aimé	j'aurais aimé
To play	jouer	joué	j'aurais joué
To dance	danser	dansé	j'aurais dansé

2nd Group Verbs:

Verb	Infinitive	Past Participle	Conditional Perfect (I)

	tive	ple	
To finish	finir	fini	j'aurais fini
To choose	choisir	choisi	j'aurais choisi
To succeed	réussir	réussi	j'aurais réussi

3rd Group Verbs:

Verb	Infinitive	Past Participle	Conditional Perfect (I)
To go	aller	allé	je serais allé(e)
T	pre	pris	j'aurais pris

o t a k e	ndr e		
T o s e e	voi r	vu	j'aurais vu

7.6 Exercises

To reinforce your understanding, here are some exercises:

19. Conjugate the verb "aimer" in the present perfect tense.
20. Conjugate the verb "finir" in the pluperfect tense.
21. Conjugate the verb "aller" in the future perfect tense.
22. Conjugate the verb "prendre" in the conditional perfect tense.

Chapter 8: Non-Personal Forms

8.1 Infinitive

The infinitive is the base form of the verb, often used after another verb or a preposition. Here are some examples:

Verb	Infinitive
To love	aimer
To finish	finir
To go	aller

Examples:

- I want to love: Je veux aimer.
- He needs to finish: Il doit finir.
- We are going to go: Nous allons aller.

8.2 Present Participle

The present participle is formed by adding -ant to the stem of the verb. It is used to form gerunds and as an adjective. Here are some examples:

Verb	Infinitive	Present Participle
To love	aimer	aimant

Verb	Infinitive	Present Participle
To finish	finir	finissant
To go	aller	allant

Examples:

- Loving: aimant
- Finishing: finissant
- Going: allant

8.3 Past Participle

The past participle is used to form compound tenses and as an adjective. Here are some examples:

Verb	Infinitive	Past Participle
To love	aimer	aimé
To finish	finir	fini
To go	aller	allé

Examples:

- Loved: aimé
- Finished: fini
- Gone: allé

8.4 Gerund

The gerund is formed by using the present participle with the preposition "en". It is used to express simultaneous actions. Here are some examples:

Verb	Infinitive	Gerund
To love	aimer	en aimant
To finish	finir	en finissant
To go	aller	en allant

Examples:

- While loving: en aimant
- While finishing: en finissant
- While going: en allant

8.5 Exercises

To reinforce your understanding, here are some exercises:

23.   Form the present participle of the verb "aimer".
24.   Form the past participle of the verb "finir".
25.   Use the gerund form of the verb "aller" in a sentence.

Chapter 9: Special Conjugations

9.1 Reflexive Verbs

Reflexive verbs are used when the subject and the object of the verb are the same. They are conjugated with reflexive pronouns. Here are some examples:

Verb	Infinitive	Present (I)	Past (I)	Future (I)
To wash oneself	se lav er	je me lave	je me suis lavé(e)	je me laverai
To get up	se lev er	je me lèv e	je me suis levé(e)	je me lèverai
To dress oneself	s' h a bi	je m' ha bill	je me suis habillé(e)	je m'h abill erai

ll	e	
er		

Examples:

- I wash myself: je me lave
- You got up: tu t'es levé(e)
- He will dress himself: il s'habillera

9.2 Impersonal Verbs

Impersonal verbs are used only in the third person singular and do not refer to a specific subject. Here are some examples:

Verb	Infinitive	Present (It)	Past (It)	Future (It)
To rain	ple uv oir	il pleut	il a pl u	il pleu vra
To be necessary	fall oir	il faut	il a fa llu	il fau dra

Examples:

- It rains: il pleut
- It was necessary: il a fallu
- It will rain: il pleuvra

9.3 Defective Verbs

Defective verbs are verbs that are not conjugated in all tenses or forms. Here are some examples:

Verb	Infinitive	Present (I)	Past (I)	Future (I)
To be able to	pouvoir	je peux	j'ai pu	je pourrai
To know	savoir	je sais	j'ai su	je saurai

Examples:

- I can: je peux
- I knew: j'ai su
- I will know: je saurai

9.4 Exercises

To reinforce your understanding, here are some exercises:

26. Conjugate the reflexive verb "se laver" in the present tense.
27. Conjugate the impersonal verb "pleuvoir" in the past tense.
28. Conjugate the defective verb "pouvoir" in the future tense.

Chapter 10: Exercises and Practice

10.1 Introduction to Exercises

Exercises are essential for reinforcing your understanding and mastery of French conjugation. This chapter provides a series of exercises covering different groups of verbs and tenses studied in previous chapters.

10.2 Exercises on 1st Group Verbs

Exercise 1: Conjugate the following verbs in the present tense.

Verb	I	You (singular)	He/She/It	We	You (plural)	They
To sing	je chant	tu chantes	il/elle chant	nous chantons	vous chantez	ils/elles chantent

	e		e			
To play	je joue	tu joues	il/elle joue	nous jouons	vous jouez	ils/elles jouent
To dance	je danse	tu danses	il/elle danse	nous dansons	vous dansez	ils/elles dansent

Exercise 2: Conjugate the following verbs in the past tense.

Verb	I	You (singular)	He/She/It	We	You (plural)	They
To	j'	tu as	il/elle	nous	vous	ils/elle

love

aimé	aimé	elle a aimé	avons aimé	avez aimé	ont aimé

To speak

j'ai parlé	tu as parlé	il/elle a parlé	nous avons parlé	vous avez parlé	ils/elles ont parlé

To watch

j'ai regardé	tu as regardé	il/elle a regardé	nous avons regardé	vous avez regardé	ils/elles ont regardé

10.3 Exercises on 2nd Group Verbs

Exercise 3: Conjugate the following verbs in the imperfect tense.

Verb	I	You (singular)	He/She/It	We	You (plural)	They
To finish	je finissais	tu finissais	il/elle finissait	nous finissions	vous finissiez	ils/elles finissaient
To choose	je choisi	tu choississais	il/elle choisissait	nous choissions	vous choisissiez	ils/elles choisissaient

Verb	je	tu	il/elle	nous	vous	ils/elles
e	ssais					
To succeed	je réussissais	tu réussissais	il/elle réussissait	nous réussissions	vous réussissiez	ils/elles réussissaient

Exercice 4: Conjugate the following verbs in the future tense.

Verb	I	You (singular)	He/She/It	We	You (plural)	They

)

	je	tu	il/elle	nous	vous	ils/elles
To grow (grandir)	je grandirai	tu grandiras	il/elle grandira	nous grandirons	vous grandirez	ils/elles grandiront
To applaud (applaudir)	j'applaudirai	tu applaudiras	il/elle applaudira	nous applaudirons	vous applaudirez	ils/elles applaudiront
To b r	je r	tu rougi	il/elle ro	nous rougir	vous roug	ils/elles rou

l	o	ra	ug	ons	ire	giro
u	u	s	ir		z	nt
s	g		a			
h	i					
	r					
	a					
	i					

10.4 Exercises on 3rd Group Verbs

Exercise 5: Conjugate the following verbs in the present subjunctive.

Verb	That I	That you (singular)	That he/she/it	That we	That you (plural)	That they
To sell	que je vend	que tu vendes	qu'il / elle vend en	que nous vendions	que vous vendiez	qu'ils/elles vendent

e	de			

To receive

que je reçoive

que tu reçoives	qu'il/elle reçoive	que nous recevions	que vous receviez	qu'ils/elles reçoivent

To leave

que je parte

que tu partes	qu'il/elle parte	que nous partions	que vous partiez	qu'ils/elles partent

Exercise 6: Conjugate the following verbs in the conditional present.

Verb	I	You (si	He/She	We	You (p	They
		Yo u (si	H e/ Sh	W e	Y ou (p	The y

b		ng ul ar)	e/ lt		lu ra l)	
To take	je prendrais	tu prendrais	il/elle prendrait	nous prendrions	vous prendriez	ils/elles prendraient
To drink	je boirais	tu boirais	il/elle boirait	nous boirions	vous boiriez	ils/elles boiraient
To live	je vivrais	tu vivrais	il/elle vivrait	nous vivrions	vous vivriez	ils/elles vivraient

e	a	t
	i	
	s	

10.5 Exercises on Irregular Verbs

Exercise 7: Conjugate the following verbs in the present tense.

Verb	I	You (singular)	He/She/He/It	We	You (plural)	They
To be	je suis	tu es	il / elle est	nous sommes	vous êtes	ils / elles sont
To have	j'ai	tu as	il / elle a	nous avons	vous avez	ils / elles ont
T	j	tu	il	nou	vo	ils

o	e	vas	/	s	us	/e
			el	allo	all	lle
g	v		le	ns	ez	s
o	a		v			vo
	i		a			nt
	s					

Exercise 8: Conjugate the following verbs in the past tense.

Verb	I	You (singular)	He/She/It	We	You (plural)	They
Todo	j'ai fait	tu as fait	il/elle a fait	nous avons fait	vous avez fait	ils/elles ont fait
Tobea	j'ai	tu as pu	il/elle	nous avons pu	vous avez pu	ils/elles ont pu

bl e t o	p u		a p u		
T o w a n t	j' a i v o u l u	tu as vo ul u	il / e ll e a v o u l u	nou s avo ns vou lu	vo us av ez vo ulu	ils/ ell es ont vou lu

10.6 Exercises on Compound Tenses

Exercise 10: Conjugate the following verbs in the future perfect tense.

V e r b	I	Y o u (s i n	H e/ Sh e/ It	We	Yo u (pl ura l)	The y

	g u l a r)				
To come	je serai venu(e)	tu seras venu(e)	il/elle sera venu(e)	nous serons venu(e)s	vous serez venu(e)(s)	ils/elles seront venu(e)s
To leave	je serai parti(e)	tu seras parti(e)	il/elle sera parti(e)	nous serons parti(e)s	vous serez parti(e)(s)	ils/elles seront parti(e)s

)

	j' aurai fait	tu auras fait	il/elle aura fait	nous aurons fait	vous aurez fait	ils/elles auront fait
Todo						

10.7 Conclusion of the Chapter

This chapter provided a series of practical exercises to reinforce your understanding and mastery of French conjugation. By practicing regularly, you will be able to consolidate your knowledge and improve your proficiency in French.

Chapter 11: Appendices

11.1 List of Irregular Verbs

Here is a list of common irregular verbs and their conjugations:

Verb	Infinitive	Present (I)	Past (I)	Future (I)

To be	être	je suis	j'ai été	je serai
To have	avoir	j'ai	j'ai eu	j'aurai
To go	aller	je vais	je suis allé(e)	j'irai
To do	faire	je fais	j'ai fait	je ferai
To take	prendre	je prends	j'ai pris	je prendrai
To see	voir	je vois	j'ai vu	je verrai

e

11.2 Summary Tables

Here are summary tables for the conjugation patterns of regular verbs:

1st Group Verbs (ending in -er):

Tense	I	You (singular)	He/She/It	We	You (plural)	They
Present	-e	-es	-e	-ons	-ez	-ent
Past	-é	-é	-é	-é	-é	-é
Future	-erai	-eras	-era	-erons	-erez	-eront

2nd Group Verbs (ending in -ir):

Tense	I	You (singular)	He/She/It	We	You (plural)	They
Present	-is	-is	-it	-issons	-issez	-issent
Past	-i	-i	-i	-i	-i	-i
Future	-irai	-iras	-ira	-irons	-irez	-iront

3rd Group Verbs (irregular):

Tense	I	You (singular)	He/She/It	We	You (plural)	They
Present	varies	varies	varies	varies	varies	varies
Past	varies	varies	varies	varies	varies	varies
Future	varies	varies	varies	varies	varies	varies

Chapter 12: Verbs with Particles

12.1 Definition and Characteristics

Verbs with particles are verbs that are combined with prepositions or adverbs to create a new meaning. Here are some examples:

Verb	Infinitive	Present (I)	Past (I)	Future (I)
To get up	se lever	je me lève	je me suis levé(e)	je me lèverai
To wake up	se réveiller	je me réveille	je me suis réveillé(e)	je me réveillerai
To sit down	s'asseoir	je m'assieds	je me suis assis(e)	je m'assiérai

Examples:

- I get up: je me lève
- You woke up: tu t'es réveillé(e)
- He will sit down: il s'assiéra

12.2 Conjugation Patterns

The conjugation patterns for verbs with particles follow the same rules as regular and irregular verbs, but include the reflexive pronouns. Here are some examples:

Se lever (to get up):

Pronoun	Present	Past	Future
I	me lève	me suis levé(e)	me lèverai
You (singular)	te lèves	t'es levé(e)	te lèveras
He/She/It	se lève	s'est levé(e)	se lèver

			a
We	nous levons	nous sommes levé(e)s	nous lèverons
You (plural)	vous levez	vous êtes levé(e)(s)	vous lèverez
They	se lèvent	se sont levé(e)s	se lèveront

S'asseoir (to sit down):

Pronoun	Present	Past	Future
I	m'assieds	me suis assis(e)	m'assiérai
You (singular)	t'assieds	t'es assis(e)	t'assiéras
He/She/It	s'assied	s'est assis(e)	s'assiéra
We	nous asseyons	nous sommes	nous assiér

	ons	assis(e)s	ons
You (plur al)	vous assey ez	vous êtes assis(e)(s)	vous assiér ez
They	s'ass eyent	se sont assis(e)s	s'assi éront

12.3 Exercices

To reinforce your understanding, here are some exercises:

29. Conjugate the verb "se lever" in the present tense.
30. Conjugate the verb "se réveiller" in the past tense.
31. Conjugate the verb "s'asseoir" in the future tense.

Chapter 13: Conclusion

13.1 Summary of Key Points

Throughout this manual, we have explored various aspects of French conjugation, detailing the rules and exceptions for each group of verbs and each tense. Here is a summary of the key points covered:

- **Chapters 1 to 3**: Introduction to the 1st, 2nd, and 3rd group verbs, with conjugation tables for each tense of the indicative.
- **Chapter 4**: Irregular verbs, their peculiarities, and their specific conjugations.
- **Chapter 5**: Indicative tenses, including the present, imperfect, past perfect, pluperfect, future simple, and future perfect.

- **Chapter 6**: The subjunctive, its uses, and its conjugations.
- **Chapter 7**: Compound tenses, their formation, and their use.
- **Chapter 8**: Non-personal forms, including the infinitive, participle, and gerund.
- **Chapter 9**: Special conjugations, such as reflexive, impersonal, and defective verbs.
- **Chapter 10**: Practical exercises to reinforce understanding and mastery of conjugations.
- **Chapter 11**: Appendices, including lists of irregular verbs and summary tables.
- **Chapter 12**: Verbs with particles, their formation, and their use.

13.2 Encouragement for Continued Practice

Mastering French conjugation is an ongoing process that requires regular practice and constant review. Here are some tips to help you continue to progress:

32. **Practice Regularly**: Dedicate time each day to conjugating verbs. Use apps, exercise books, or websites to vary your resources.
33. **Read in French**: Reading books, articles, or newspapers in French will help you see conjugations in context and reinforce your understanding.
34. **Write in French**: Keep a journal, write letters, or emails in French to practice writing and using different tenses and moods.
35. **Speak in French**: Engage in conversations with native speakers or join discussion groups to practice speaking.
36. **Review Regularly**: Revisit previous chapters and redo exercises to consolidate your knowledge.

The key to success lies in perseverance and continuous practice. Every effort you make brings you closer to mastering the French language. Keep practicing, learning, and improving. Good luck on

Made in the USA
Las Vegas, NV
21 October 2024